A Murmuration

Adam Colclough

Cover Art by

A Blind Photographer

A MURMURATION

First Printing: 2024

ISBN: 978-1-7394900-2-7 (DREAM WELL WRITING)
DREAM WELL WRITING LTD
STAFFORDSHIRE
UNITED KINGDOM

www.dreamwellwriting.simplesite.com

Typeset in Verdana

A Dyslexia Friendly Publication

DEDICATION

In memory of my late parents William and Barbara Colclough

ACKNOWLEDGEMENTS

I would like to thank the following for making this book possible:

Mel Wardle Woodend and Dream Well for giving me the opportunity to see my poems appear in a 'for real' book.

The proprietors of Captain's Bar and WordCraft at BottleCraft in Hanley for giving me a platform to perform my poems, and Newcastle Common, Appetite and B-Arts for all the hard work they do to promote the arts in my hometown.

You have all played a part in helping these little birds take flight, for which I will always be grateful.

CONTENTS

A Love Heart is not a Swastika

A love heart is not a swastika.
No army crossed the border at
dawn
with its flag to the fore,
the gutters aren't filled with
glass
where hearts get painted on
walls.
No cruel September saw
fields sown with blood in their
name.
Their pinkness stands only
for the warmth of being
alive.
Do not shout; do not
cry,
a love heart, is not a swastika.

November 2017

Bottle Kiln

By the canal, your
curve
lost in a stylish
nowhere
reminds those
passing that
this spot was once
loud with work.

The art, captive
in rough hands
shaping
Earth
forms.
Simple. Folk
remembered
as carved
names,
erased by rain.

July 2018

Brambles

Growing through
the garden's neatness,
a vacant plot
where the factory stood.

An old enemy,
fought by soft hands,
their efforts shameful
to peasant forebears.

When humans finally
blow themselves into fragments,
the brambles will come.
Reclaiming our ruins
with berries, dark
as martyr's blood.

August 2018

Sample

A sharp scratch draws
almost an armful,
that is
undeniably mine.

This is immortality,
in a whole new way.
A smear on glass
outliving
the thin shadow
I cast.

Mocking chapel promises

made in innocence of

spirit,

the day, world and city

belong

to cells dividing,

knowing no purpose

but their own.

December 2017

Sea Defences

Waves worry the fragile

        shore

                anger older than time

                        playing with our

                island

        like a fat ginger tom

playing with a mouse.

        Men are not mice

                they arrogantly

                        refuse

                to make the ancient

        compromise.

They build bulwarks

        against

                the fall into a vortex

                        all life travels towards

                what survives our little

        hour

will not be, the soaring

cathedral so much,

as these buried

attempts

at turning back,

the tide.

March 2018

A Murmuration

Above stark fields
turning as one
small lives in
unison,

a pattern, wonder
enough to see,
still more to think
on

surely evidence
a larger hand,
shaped our ordinary
clay

the spirit we trap,
behind stained glass;
breaking free,

to turn deftly in air,
mocking, mortal
unimaginative, man.

March 2017

The Thief in the Candle

Life, like a candle,

hides

flaws behind perfection.

Showing when

lit,

the hidden fault,

making

its light grow dim.

Presented as

wax,

revealed as tallow all

along.

Life's guttering light

is all we have;

and the night is so

long.

June 2018

Vessel

Formed in fire,

a simple cup

filled with new

wine.

Passed to the right,

down through

time.

A rough draught

slaking the oldest thirst.

July 2017

Visitors

Softly whispering,

they come at dusk

to homes, packed

together in grey towns

marking a life, sailing

upriver to its end.

A sort of comfort

failing to drive off

what we know

and most fear knowing:

that in time,

each house is visited.

September 2018

House Clearance

Time empties

lives

like cheap suitcases.

Once known things

form

awkward new pairings,

mocking their lost

certainties.

The slow, sure

dissolving

of who we were

into just what we

had,

too little to dodge

this strange, priced

oblivion.

May 2018

On Meeting a Funeral

My ancestor, coming from his
labour
would have crossed himself,
warding off a fear known too well.

I stand dumb, awkward,
caught out by black cars
absorbing light;
giving back
a draught from closed
rooms.

Science provides distance
from the dark guest at every
hearth.
The ragged witch bringing
her gift to each hurried
churching.

Like the ape we missed,
in that film they showed
in first year psych, she capers
at the edge of our sight.

What good is our science,
when the pills
stop
working?
Formulae are only prayers
offered up to angry gods.
Reason holds firm, breaking.
In the wind, superstition rides
out.

Maybe this line of cars
carrying
modern people to old rites,
will become more than an
awkward game.

Shape instead into a
strong reminder
that we are all fragile.
Reaching always for the
stars.
Knowing we return to
Earth.

August 2017

Little Albert

Screams echoing in the
abandoned hospital,
backwards to the sun
streaming in
at arched windows
on the monkey who
thought
he was born to lead
a march into utopia.

Progress always demands
blood.
Science claims as its
sacrifice
the innocence of
yesterday,
a parade of expandable
dolls in wire cages

turning into crowds,

roaring

in a torch-lit stadium.

You couldn't have guessed

the dark century you

brought

to its bloody birth.

Its bombs and

barracks

a homage to apes,

too clever to be good.

March 2018

From a Window, Autumn

Leaves fuss dirty glass,
I look down on Station Road
at taxis huddling
in thin drizzle.

Trains run to Manchester,
remote as Pluto on this grey day.
Behind me the half-lit library
swells,
ideas crouch, waiting
to disrupt minds closed at
school.

Somewhere a door slams,
like swearing in church.
The trains rush on to
somewhere,
as the taxis patiently wait

for strangers to reach a new

here.

Nothing happens, the world

grows

one whole hour older,

as we all pretend not to

notice.

This is what it feels like,

standing still, as everything else

turns.

I step back into familiar,

book crowded dimness;

that demands less

than love.

October 2017

Blast

Years, the shell slept

in earth bought with blood.

Long enough to forget

munitions girls, flirting with boys,

a King Emperor sent to fight

his cousin for a field.

Woken; its voice became

the roar of men pressed

under white stones, calling

out for their lost years.

September 2017

ABOUT THE AUTHOR

Adam Colclough was born in Stoke-on-Trent, Staffordshire and is a graduate of Staffordshire University. He is a regular contributor of articles and reviews to Shots magazine and Central Bylines.

DREAM WELL WRITING LTD

Dream Well Writing Ltd are Staffordshire based publishers of dyslexia friendly books – with worldwide distribution and an environmentally conscious ethos – founded in 2017 by Mel Wardle Woodend Staffordshire Poet Laureate 2019 – 2022.

Books by Dream Well Writing are produced responsibly using acid free inks, recycled paper and a print on demand service to reduce waste from excess copies.

Find out more about Dream Well at

http://dreamwellwriting.simplesite.com/

https://www.facebook.com/dreamwellwriting/

dreamwellwriting@gmail.com

Printed in Great Britain
by Amazon

41553791R00020